iParenting Media Award

A Parents' Choice selection

"Offers youngsters an alternative to hitting
and other forms of hurtful behavior."
—*School Library Journal*

"The simple but important message...helps children understand
that they have the power to choose not to hurt people."
—*Teaching Tolerance*

Hands Are Not for Hitting

Martine Agassi, Ph.D.

Illustrations by Marieka Heinlen

free spirit
PUBLiSHiNG®

Helping kids
help themselves™
since 1983

Text copyright © 2000 by Martine Agassi, Ph.D.
Illustrations copyright © 2000 by Marieka Heinlen

Free Spirit, Free Spirit Publishing, and associated logos are trademarks and/or registered trademarks of Free Spirit Publishing Inc. A complete listing of our logos and trademarks is available at www.freespirit.com.

Library of Congress Cataloging-in-Publication Data
Agassi, Martine, 1966–
    Hands are not for hitting / Martine Agassi ; illustrations by Marieka Heinlen.
        p.   cm.
    Summary: Demonstrates that "hands are not for hitting" by suggesting many positive uses for them, such as saying hello, playing, creating, and helping.
    ISBN 1-57542-077-5 (pbk.)
     1. School violence—Prevention—Juvenile literature. 2. Anger—Juvenile literature. 3. Hand—Juvenile literature. 4. Early childhood education—Activity programs—Juvenile literature. [1. Behavior. 2. Anger. 3. Violence.] I. Heinlen, Marieka, ill. II. Title.
    LB3013.3 .A33 2000
    372.17'82—dc21

                                                        00-022627

At the time of this book's publication, all facts and figures cited are the most current available; all telephone numbers, addresses, and Web site URLs are accurate and active; all publications, organizations, Web sites, and other resources exist as described in this book; and all have been verified as of June 2005. The author and Free Spirit Publishing make no warranty or guarantee concerning the information and materials given out by organizations or content found at Web sites, and we are not responsible for any changes that occur after this book's publication. If you find an error or believe that a resource listed here is not as described, please contact Free Spirit Publishing. Parents, teachers, and other adults: We strongly urge you to monitor children's use of the Internet.

"Hands Are Not for Hitting" is the registered trademark of the Minnesota Coalition for Battered Women, and is used with permission.

Cover and interior design by Marieka Heinlen
Edited by Marjorie Lisovskis and Elizabeth Verdick

20 19 18 17 16 15 14 13 12 11 10 9
Printed in Hong Kong

Free Spirit Publishing Inc.
217 Fifth Avenue North, Suite 200
Minneapolis, MN 55401-1299
(612) 338-2068
help4kids@freespirit.com
www.freespirit.com

To J.C., whose faithfulness in my life gives me purpose, strength, and peace

A portion of proceeds from the sales of this book will be donated to the Andre Agassi Foundation, which lends a helping hand to children in need or at risk.

Acknowledgments

A sincere and heartfelt thank-you to my editors, Elizabeth Verdick and Margie Lisovskis. You've made my work effortless and transformed my ideas into simple brilliance. To the talented Marieka Heinlen, thank you for capturing the playfulness and innocence of how childhood should be for every child. And to Judy Galbraith, my publisher, thank you for your belief in the book.

Grateful acknowledgment goes to the Minnesota Coalition for Battered Women for their insightful contributions to the book and for allowing the use of the book's title.

Thanks to teacher Patti Loftus for her careful review of the manuscript.

Many thanks to my mentors, Dr. Norton Roitman and Dr. Crista Peterson.

Thank you to Andre; you'll never know the extent to which your generosity has enriched the lives of our family.

To my best friends, Kirsten and Joe; your love and loyalty embody true friendship. Thank you for the many gifts of your friendship.

Forever thanks to my parents, Mona and Jack. Amongst so much, you've always been my safety net. My gratitude overflows.

To my daughter, Carter, God's love is ever present in you. Thank you for making my heart smile.

Finally, to my husband, Phillip, thank you for always encouraging my every dream. Because of you, I've become a better person.

Dear Grown-Ups,

It's a great privilege to be involved in the life of a child, whether as a parent, stepparent, teacher, child-care provider, group leader, or friend. It's also an awesome responsibility. Part of our job as caring adults is to instill and nurture values that will guide the child now and in the future. One of the most important values is a commitment to peaceful actions and nonviolence.

We must help children know and understand that violence is never okay, and that they are capable of constructive, loving actions—of making good choices. These are the central themes of *Hands Are Not for Hitting*. These themes go hand-in-hand with messages of love, kindness, acceptance, responsibility, patience, encouragement, perseverance, honor, and loyalty. All children can learn to use their hands to care for themselves and others.

Hands Are Not for Hitting is meant to be read aloud—to one child, a group, or a class. It gives simple, straightforward reasons why hitting is harmful and unhealthy. It encourages children to think about and practice behaviors that build a sense of self-esteem, self-awareness, respect, caring, responsibility, and fun.

At the end of the book, you'll find background information, ideas for more activities to do together, and resources that support and expand the book's message.

I hope you'll share this book again and again to reinforce children's understanding and appreciation of their own abilities. Emphasize that all children have the power to use their hands—and the rest of their body—in positive ways.

A big hand to you!

Love,

Marti

Hands come in all shapes, sizes, and colors.
There are lots of things your hands are meant to do.

Hands are for saying hello.

Hands are for greeting and communicating.

You can wave to a friend.

You can shake hands when
you meet someone.

Waving or shaking hands shows
that you want to be friendly.

Try it now. Shake hands with the person next to you.

You can draw
and write words . . .

and send a message
to someone you love.

There are many friendly
ways you can use your hands
to communicate.

I can tell a
story with
my hands.

This means
"butterfly."

There's something that hands are NOT for.

Hands are not for hitting.
Hitting isn't friendly.
Hitting hurts.

Hands are not for pushing or pinching, either.

How does it feel
when someone hits you?

It hurts your body.
It hurts your
feelings, too.

How does it feel when you hit someone else?

It hurts the person's body.
It hurts the person's
feelings, too.

Why do people hit? Sometimes they feel . . .

Sometimes they want to be the boss of other people.

Have you felt this way?

Maybe you wanted to hit someone.

But hands are not for hitting.

And feet are not for kicking.

There are other ways to let your feelings out.
You can . . .

draw a picture

write about
how you feel

squish clay
or dough

push against
the wall with
all your might

play an
instrument

jump up and down

listen to music

punch a
pillow

dig in sand

tell someone
you're upset
and talk
about it
together

We can use
our words.

Can you think of other ways to let your feelings out?

After a while, you'll feel better.

When that happens,
you and your hands
can play again.

Hands are for all kinds of playing . . .

alone   and together

You can have a lot of fun. You can . . .

make finger
shadows

play puppets

make silly faces

blow bubbles that
float to the sky

make
mud pies

How do you use *your* hands to play?

Hands are for making music.

For playing a song

snapping

clapping

or tapping out a beat.

Can you tap your fingers? Give it a try!

Hands are for working together.
You can build . . .

snowpeople

a sandcastle

a block tower

triple-scoop sundaes with
nuts and a cherry!

Hands are for playing, learning, doing, and building.

Hands are not for hitting. Hitting is never okay.

So what can you do when you and your
friend aren't getting along?

You can try to solve the problem together.

You can talk about it.

You can listen.

You can try to understand how your friend feels.

Your friend can try to understand how *you* feel, too.

You can think of ways to make things right.

What if your friend yells, kicks, pushes, or hits?
You don't have to fight back.

You can walk away.

You can find something else to do,
or someone else to play with,
or an older person who can help.

I'll talk to my teacher.

I could ask my mom.

Grandpa could help me.

Maybe my sister has an idea.

You can tell your friend, "Hands are not for hitting."

Hands are for helping.

There are many ways you can use your hands to be a helper. You can . . .

make your bed

feed your pet

share your toys and put them away.

You can set the table.

You can help your little brother get dressed.

How do you make yourself handy?

I help carry groceries.

I match socks!

We clean up after a spill.

Hands are also for taking care of *you*.

They're for dressing

and undressing . . .

eating and drinking.

They're for washing your face,
combing your hair, brushing your teeth . . .

and turning out
the light at
bedtime.

brusha brusha brusha . . .

What do you do to take care of *you*?

Hands are for keeping safe.

You hold a grown-up's hand when you cross the street.

You buckle your seat belt when you ride in a car.

You put on your helmet when you ride a bike.

Think of all the ways your hands can keep you safe!

Hands are for helping. Hands are for caring.

Hands are for keeping you healthy and safe.

Hands are not for hitting.

Hands are for being kind and showing love . . .

with a hug

a pat on the back

a promise

Go ahead—high five the person next to you!

Hands are also for saying good-bye.

You can blow a kiss.

You can give a little wave with your finger.

You can give a GREAT BIG wave.

A Word to Grown-Ups About Children and Violence

In teaching nonviolence to children, we need to be aware of the conflicting messages children receive from a variety of sources. Violence is deeply imbedded in our culture. All of us—children and adults—see violence on television, in movies, and in video games. We hear it in music. We observe it in others and may experience it firsthand. Sadly, many children experience physical or sexual abuse at the hands of adults.

Experts tell us that adults who abuse often believe they're entitled to have *power* over others. Feeling powerless in some aspects of their lives, they learn to use violence as a way to gain control. These beliefs and feelings begin during childhood. Thus, in teaching children about *why* people hit, the issue of power is an important one. As adults, we can help children feel empowered to make positive choices about how they'll treat others.

Yet, if children are to make choices, they must believe that they *have* choices. *Hands Are Not for Hitting* is a tool you can use to help children start to understand that they *do* have the power to choose not to hurt people. The book offers a way to begin teaching children to feel empathy toward others, to solve problems, to control negative impulses, and to cope with intense feelings like anger and jealousy in constructive ways.

You can support this message as you read and talk about the book. You can guide children in other ways, too. How? By forming warm, caring relationships with them. By setting limits that are clear and consistent. By providing consequences that are helpful and constructive. And by modeling and expressing your belief that there are alternatives to violence, that violence rarely solves problems and usually creates new ones, and that violence is not entertaining or fun. Simply put, that hitting people is *never* okay.

Ways to Reinforce Children's Understanding of *Hands Are Not for Hitting*

Pages 2–5

Hello Hands

Talk about other ways people use hands to say hello: with a salute or a peace sign, in sign language, or by cupping both hands around a person's hands. Try the different types of greetings.

Special Greetings

Come up with your own special hand greeting, such as latching pinkie fingers or grasping arms.

Friendly Hands

Talk about ways people can be friendly with their hands—playing hand games like pat-a-cake, playing circle games, holding hands to dance.

Communication Explanation

Explain the meaning of the word *communicate*: to use words and actions (such as writing or drawing) to tell someone something. Explain that we also communicate feelings through our faces, bodies, and tone of voice.

Colorful Names

Use crayons, markers, watercolors, or finger paints to write your names.

Sign Language

Use charades, picture drawings, or sign language to communicate actions such as eating, sleeping, or building. (For a reference book on sign language, see "Learn More About It," page 35.)

Talking Hands

Talk about different ways we use hands to talk.

Emotion in Motion

Use your hands, faces, and bodies to show different feelings.

Pages 6–11

Hitting Hurts

Talk about the ways hitting hurts: It hurts people's bodies and feelings. It hurts both the person being hit and the person who does the hitting. Talk about why people sometimes want to hit—because they may feel angry or upset about someone or something.

Feeling Faces

Together, think of as many words for feelings as you can. Have children draw or make a face to correspond to each feeling.

Feelings Chart

Make a chart children or family members can use to show how they're feeling. On self-stick notes, draw simple faces showing different feelings. Write children's or family members' names across the top. Tell children they can use their hands to stick a note showing how they feel under their name on the chart.

Handling Feelings

Tell children that it's okay to have strong feelings like anger, jealousy, or fear. There are acceptable ways to show these feelings and to help them go away—ways that are safe and that don't hurt people. Discuss the ideas suggested and also encourage children to suggest other ways to deal with intense feelings.

Pages 12–16

Hand Hunt

Put objects in a box or bag, then close your eyes and use your hands to identify them.

Fingerprint Fun

Make fingerprint pictures using a washable inkpad and paper. Notice how each fingerprint is different from the rest. Turn your fingerprints into faces, raindrops, falling leaves, or stars.

No Hands

Put your hands behind your back for five minutes. See what it's like not to be able to use your hands as you talk, play, or work.

Paired Hands

Put one hand in your pocket and keep it there. Then try to create a clay creature or a block structure using only one hand. Or work in pairs, each person using one hand so that together you have two hands. Try a similar activity using a single hand or two people's paired hands to play an instrument or paint a picture. Talk about how two people working together can create something fun and unique. What if the two people decided to fight instead of work together? There would be two angry people and no building, music, or painting.

Cooperating Hands

Take time to discuss the many ways people use their hands to play, learn, and work together.

Pages 17–19

Solving Problems

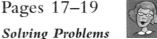

Ask: **Have you and a friend had a problem to solve? What happened?** Discuss or role-play situations where children might need to solve a problem. Come up with different ideas for solving the problem.

Avoiding Fights

Encourage children to think of different things to do in order to get away from fighting or other violence. Help children identify different adults who can help them.

Pages 20–21

Helping Hands

Use your hands to pantomime the helping activities described. Talk about other ways people help and work, and pantomime some of these as well. Ask: **What are some things you do to help at home? At school? What are some ways people help *you*? What are some other things you can do to be helpful?**

Pages 22–23

Helping Ourselves

Talk about and pantomime the many things people do each day to take care of themselves: sleeping, getting exercise, grooming, eating healthy foods.

Pages 24–25

Staying Safe

Talk about and pantomime different ways to be safe.

"No" Talk

An important part of children's safety is knowing what to do when another child or an older person tries to get them to do something that doesn't feel right. Tell children that they can say "no" in a big voice, run away to a safe place, and tell an adult they trust about what happened.

Talk about the kinds of things children say "no" to (fighting, being mean to others, dangerous play). Encourage children to find words as well as hand and body gestures for saying "no."

Help children identify trusted adults they can talk to about things that feel wrong to them.

Ask: **What are some things you don't like to do or that feel wrong to you? What are some ways to say "no"?** ("Stop it." "I don't want to play like that." "I don't feel like doing that." "I feel angry about that." "NO.") **Who can you tell when something feels wrong to you?**

Feeling Safe at Home

Children also need to know that they have safe recourse from violence in their own home. Here are four ideas you can share with children:

---

4 Things Children Can Do If There Is Fighting at Home

1. Plan a safe place where you can go when the fighting starts.
2. Go to your safe place and draw pictures, read, or play a game.
3. If you don't feel safe, call 911. Tell the operator your name and address and that there's a fight going on.
4. Talk about the fighting with a grown-up you trust. If you can't get help at home, talk to a grandparent, an aunt, an uncle, a teacher, a caregiver, or a leader at your place of worship.

As an adult, you may also find the following helpful:

4 Things Adults Can Do If There Is Fighting at Home

1. Call 911.
2. Call a local shelter hotline.
3. Talk with a family counselor, therapist, or clergy person. Your child's school counselor may also be able to refer you for help. If cost is a concern, let the counselor know. Low-cost or free services are often available. Keep looking for someone to help until you find a person or an organization who can help you.
4. Stay with friends or family.

NOTE: If you suspect that a child is being abused, contact your local Social Service Department, Child Welfare Department, Police Department, or District Attorney's Office. If you teach in a public or private school setting, consult first with your school principal or director to learn the established course of action.

Pages 26–27
Kindly Hands

Talk about the many ways people can use their hands to show kindness and love. When talking about hugging, emphasize that hugging feels good when both people want the hug. It's important for children to know that they can say "no" to a hug and that it's often appropriate to ask others if they want a hug. Ask: **What does it mean to be kind? What are some ways to show kindness to people? How do you feel when someone is kind to you? Who are some people who love you? How do they show their love? Who are some people you love? How can you show that you love them?**

Promising Hands

Explain the meaning of the word *promise*: something you say you'll do and then do for sure.

Invite children to show the different ways people make promises using their hands. Come up with some new hand gestures for making a promise to someone.

If it's appropriate in your setting, you may also want to talk with children about using hands for prayer.

> **NOTE:** Be sensitive to cultural differences regarding hand signals. For example, to many Americans, a thumbs-up means things are going well; to some Australians, though, the same signal is seen as an obscene gesture.

Pages 28–31
Good-Bye Hands

Make up your own special hand signal for saying good-bye.

Learn More About It

The following books are resources you can use on your own or with children:

Hello! Good-Bye by Aliki (New York: Greenwillow Books, 1996). A book about the many ways people around the world say hello and good-bye.

Hello Toes! Hello Feet! by Ann Whitford Paul, illustrated by Nadine Bernard Westcott (New York: DK Publishing, 1998). A playful interactive book that celebrates all the things *feet* can do.

A Safe Place by Maxine Trottier, illustrated by Judith Friedman (Morton Grove, IL: Albert Whitman & Co., 1997). Recommended for ages 5 and up, this is a simply written book, told from a child's viewpoint, about a mother and child who leave an abusive home situation to live in a shelter.

Simple Signs and *More Simple Signs* by Cindy Wheeler (New York: Puffin, 1997 and New York: Viking Children's Books, 1998). Fun, interactive books that teach American Sign Language for words familiar to young children (*cat, tiger, yes,*

play, please) using clear pictures and hints ("like peeling a banana," "like pedaling a bike") for how to make them.

We Can Get Along and *A Leader's Guide to We Can Get Along* by Lauren Murphy Payne and Claudia Rohling (Minneapolis: Free Spirit Publishing, 1997). The children's book teaches essential social skills in a way that even very young children can understand. The leader's guide includes reproducible masters such as "25 Healthy Ways to Express Anger" and "20 Things to Do Instead of Hurting Someone Back." Also provides comprehensive sections for adults on "What to Do If a Child Says, 'But Mommy/Daddy Hits Me'" and "What to Do If You Suspect That a Child Is Being Abused."

Your Body Belongs to You by Cornelia Spelman, illustrated by Teri Wiedner (Morton Grove, IL: Albert Whitman & Co., 1997). Explains in simple, reassuring language that a child's body is his or her own and that it's all right to decline unwanted touch, even touch that's meant to be friendly. A note for parents suggests ways to talk to children about good and bad touching.

Other Great Books from Free Spirit's Best Behavior™ Series

Simple words and delightful full-color illustrations guide children to choose peaceful, positive behavior. Select titles are available in two versions: a durable board book for ages baby–preschool, and a longer, more in-depth paperback for ages 4–7. Kids, parents, and teachers will love these award-winning books. Each paperback: $11.95, 40 pp., color illust., 9" x 9". Each board book: $7.95, 24 pp., color illust., 7" x 7".

Tails Are Not for Pulling
Board Book
by Elizabeth Verdick,
illustrated by Marieka Heinlen.
Shows children how to love pets gently—because pets are for loving, after all! A special section includes ideas for teaching kindness to animals, activities, and discussion starters.

Tails Are Not for Pulling
Board Book
by Elizabeth Verdick,
illustrated by Marieka Heinlen.
In simple words and delightful illustrations, this book teaches the basics of kindness to animals.

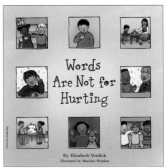

Words Are Not for Hurting
by Elizabeth Verdick,
illustrated by Marieka Heinlen.
Encourages children to think before they speak, then choose what to say and how to say it. Includes activities and discussion starters for parents and caregivers.

Feet Are Not for Kicking
Board Book
by Elizabeth Verdick,
illustrated by Marieka Heinlen.
Helps little ones learn to use their feet for fun, not in anger or frustration. Includes tips on how to help toddlers be sweet with their feet.

Teeth Are Not for Biting
Board Book
by Elizabeth Verdick,
illustrated by Marieka Heinlen.
"Crunch crunch crunch. Teeth are strong and sharp." Sooner or later, almost all young children will bite someone—a friend, parent, or sibling. This upbeat book helps prevent biting and teaches positive alternatives.

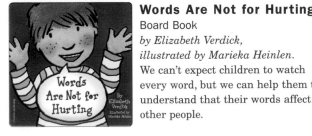

Words Are Not for Hurting
Board Book
by Elizabeth Verdick,
illustrated by Marieka Heinlen.
We can't expect children to watch every word, but we can help them to understand that their words affect other people.

Hands Are Not for Hitting
Board Book
by Martine Agassi, Ph.D.
illustrated by Marieka Heinlen.
Perfect for little hands—because it's never too early to learn that violence is never okay, hands can do many good things, and every child is capable of positive, loving actions.

To place an order or to request a free catalog of SELF-HELP FOR KIDS®
and SELF-HELP FOR TEENS® materials, please write, call, email, or visit our Web site:

Free Spirit Publishing Inc.
217 Fifth Avenue North • Suite 200 • Minneapolis, MN 55401-1299
toll-free 800.735.7323 • local 612.338.2068 • fax 612.337.5050
help4kids@freespirit.com • www.freespirit.com